To

From

Date

A RoseKidz® Rhyming Book

Precious Blessings: What Is Worship?
©2018 Valerie Marie Carpenter.

RoseKidz® is an imprint of
Rose Publishing, LLC
140 Summit Street
P.O. Box 3473
Peabody, Massachusetts 01961-3473
www.hendricksonrose.com

Book cover by Chad Thompson.
Illustrations by Chad Thompson
Book layout design by Keith DeDios

ISBN: 9781628625424
RoseKidz® reorder #L50015
JUVENILE NONFICTION/Religion/Devotional & Prayer
Printed in South Korea

01   4.2018.APC

What Is Worship?

Valerie Marie Carpenter

ROSEKiDZ®

What Is Worship?

What does it mean to worship God?
Well, I can tell you so—

It's when you tell God that you love him
Everywhere you go!

I will thank the LORD at all times. My lips will always praise him.
–Psalm 34:1

5

Anywhere

In a car, boat, bus, or a train,
At church or at home too,

Under the sun, moon, or the stars,
I say, "God, I love you."

My mouth is filled with praise for you. All day long I will talk about your glory.
—Psalm 71:8

However You Like

You can say it. You can pray it.
You can sing songs of praise.

You can raise your hands up and shout,
"Jesus, I love your ways!"

Shout for joy to the LORD, everyone on earth.
—Psalm 100:1

Different Ways

You can spin, dance, and clap, clap, clap!
And instruments are great!

Guitar, piano, flute, or drum,
It's time to celebrate!

My mouth is filled with praise for you.
All day long I will talk about your glory.
—Psalm 71:8

Loud or Soft

But here's the thing—remember this:
You don't have to be loud!

You can also gently whisper.
You can kneel, stand, or bow.

Come, let us bow down and worship him. Let us fall on our knees in front of the LORD our Maker.
—Psalms 95:6

Giving Thanks

Oh, how his love lasts forever!
He's faithful and he's true!

Your worship to God can look like
Saying, "God, I thank you!"

Give thanks to him and praise his name.
—Psalms 100:4

Showing Kindness

Worship is not just when you pray,
Or just when you sing songs.

It is also showing kindness . . .
To others all day long!

Love your neighbor as you love yourself.
—Matthew 22:39

17

Sharing with Others

Worship is sharing favorite things,
Or helping wounds to mend,

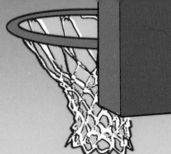

Giving food to the hungry,
Making a brand-new friend.

God is fair. He will not forget what you have done. He will remember the love you have shown him. You showed it when you helped his people. And you show it when you keep on helping them.
—Hebrews 6:10

Doing What Is Right

Worship is making good choices.
It's loving what is right.

Worship is how you live your life
Each day and every night.

The way we show our love is to obey God's commands. He commands you to lead a life of love.
—2 John 1:6

21

No Matter How You Feel

You can worship God any time,
When you feel up or down;

When you wear the biggest smile,
Or wear the saddest frown.

Always be joyful. Never stop praying.
Give thanks no matter what happens.
–1 Thessalonians 5:16-18

24

Trusting God

Worship is telling God you love him,
Even when times are tough,

When you are confused or hurting,
Say, "God, you are enough."

I will praise the Lᴏʀᴅ. Deep down inside me,
I will praise him. I will praise him,
because his name is holy.
—Psalm 103:1

Just Be Yourself

The Lord loves when you are honest,
When your worship is true.

The only thing he really wants,
Is for you to really be you!

*God is spirit. His worshipers must
worship him in the Spirit and in truth.*
—John 4:24

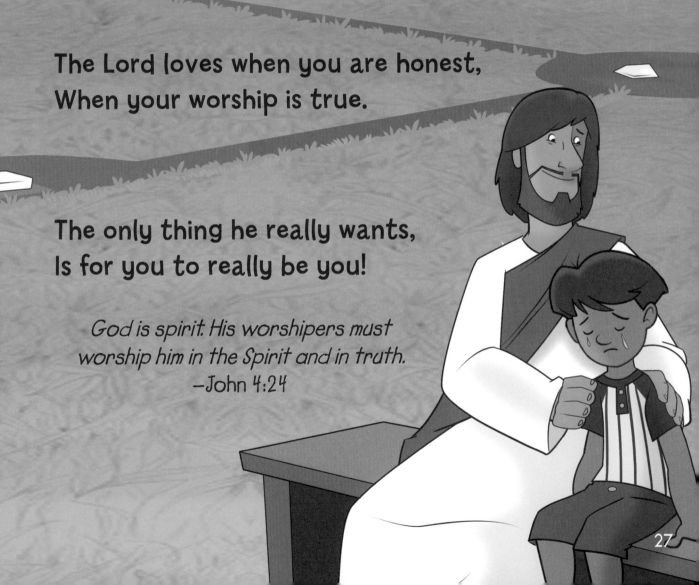

From Your Heart

So, whatever it is you do,
Or however it is you start,

Your worship to the Lord, your God,
Should come straight from your heart.

Lord my God, I will praise you with all my heart.
I will bring glory to you forever.
—Psalm 86:12

Telling God That You Love Him

So, what does it mean to worship?
Well, I think that you can say,

It's telling your God you love him
In many different ways!

Love the Lord your God with all your heart and with all your soul.
Love him with all your mind and with all your strength.
—Mark 12:30